Contents:

In Memory of:

Eric Scott Buharp

2/16/70-7/11/08

This book is dedicated to the memory of Eric Scott Buharp, to whom all my great memories and adventures are owed. Eric, I thank you for absolutely everything you have added to my life, who you have helped me to become, but most importantly for your unconditional love. No amount of words in the human language will ever be enough to express how much you are loved and missed. I will keep your memory alive until we meet again.....

2/16/70-7/11/08

Love Lives On

Reasons Behind This Manuscript:

This book was written for our boys, Hunter and Cade Buharp. I have written this to give you a hard copy of snap shots of our lives and of your daddy, especially for details you did not know or cannot remember. You always have guardians and protectors through this life-me on the earth and your daddy in heaven. May you always know how much you are loved.

Love Always,

Mom (and daddy)

My boys summer 2002

Thank You:

To friends and family that read along with the creation of this book, especially Jackie Kuehmichel. I thank you all for your friendship, love, and for traveling along this life's journey with us a little while.

Much Love,

Shannon

Chapter 1: The Beginning

I guess you could say my life began when I met Eric Buharp. Obviously, I was already alive but, I came to life. In the Spring of 1985, I was 13 years old and attended Ruckel Jr High School. I was not an outgoing student. I wasn't a cheerleader and didn't belong to any clubs. No, I guess you could say I was a wallflower.

Now don't get me wrong. I had a group of friends, most I am proud to say I am still friends with today: Lynn Sweeney, Dwana Ryals, Nicole Jones, Suzanne Finch, Jenny Reeves, Tammy Holly, Bobbi Shawn Harrison, and more.

That spring was a Ruckel dance. All 7th-9th graders could attend. I had just been allowed to start wearing makeup. The rule was 13 years old and I could, so it was purple and blue eye shadow up to my eye brows and usually jeans with three different colored crinkle socks OVER the jeans. Anyway, back to the dance.

For some reason, this dance was in the cafeteria, rather than in the usual gym. I was wearing my blue and purple eye shadow. Instead of the usual jeans, I had on a two-piece, grey pinstriped suit made of some silk-like material. I am sure it was a Bobbie Brooks special.

I saw my friends from across the room,

including my classmate Mike

Spooneybarger. Mike was standing beside the

tallest, best looking guy I had ever

seen. I would come to find out his name was

Eric Buharp. He had a smile that went

on for days and hazel eyes that twinkled and

that I swore could burn right through

me. For the love of God, even his braces were

pretty! For reasons unknown to me

to this day, he kept staring at me then walked

slowly toward me. As he was standing

before me (am I still breathing?) asks

me to dance.

I can still hear the song we danced to,

"Crazy for You" by Madonna. At the

time I had no idea that the infatuation with

this human would last a lifetime. Little did I know that our paths would cross again and again over the next 10 years. This would be a journey that now I feel certain I couldn't have lived without.

Chapter 2: Days Come and Go

In Jr. high School a few of my friends
actually got sick of me talking about him
so much, especially Lynn. In 7th grade, we
had P.E. 2nd period. Well, we just
simply could not dress out for P.E. and
participate. It was still early in the day, and
we would mess up our hair (80s big hair), so
we sat against the fence and talked,
me about Eric Buharp. I would say things
like "Lynn, I saw Eric on the way to
geography when I walked through the locker
hall. He smiled and waved at me!"
Meanwhile, Lynn would try to smile politely

while silently thinking "Gag me." She was so sick of hearing about this 9th grader.

At the second Ruckel dance, he actually kissed me. MY FIRST KISS. He laid it on me, and I swear a saw stars and heard the National Anthem play. I was dizzy, lightheaded, and remember thinking I am not sure what love is, but I am pretty sure I am in it! A few dances later and there was the occasional date to a movie. My granny ALWAYS drove me and picked me up again. I was 13, and she would give me no time for nonsense.

Another year went by, and I am in 8th grade. My favorite teacher was and still is Mrs. Deborah Mann. English was and always

will be my favorite subject. I think
this is partly because of her. She was kind to
me, and I always wanted to make her
proud. I remember once giving her a pageant
picture of me. She pinned it to the
peg board in her room for everyone to see.
That made me feel so proud. There was
something familiar about her, something that
reminded me of my mother, or rather
what I wished my mother could be for me.
My mom lived in Alabama, and I did not get
to see her very much.

Eric had moved on to 10th grade and
attended Niceville High School. He had
moved up to the BIG TIME. Niceville High
School is directly across the street

from Ruckel. Every day as I walked the ramp to Mrs. Mann's class he would be standing outside Mr. Pinter's art class and wave at me. Talk about making my day! Sometimes he would still pick me up from school in a baby blue pick up truck. He was allowed to drive me straight to my granny's house, which was approximately 0.25 miles away, and she KNEW what time school got out.

Eric got more involved in Niceville High School, 10th grade, and being a 16-year Old. I was stuck at Ruckel. Naturally he was more interested in girls that could actually GO somewhere with him. Back then instead of calling it dating, we called it *going with.* Whenever I would hear he was *going with* someone, I would get so mad I would stand in front of the full-length mirror that hung behind my granny's bedroom door, look at myself while talking to an imaginary Eric. With one hand on my hip and the other up in the air and finger waving, I'd say things like "One day you may want to have something to do with me, and I may just not have time for YOU at the moment!" So there! I told him…well, sort of…

Occasionally, he would still give me a ride to granny's house, come inside, sit on the couch with me and drink a coke from her beauty shop coke machine. I would be so excited! I truly wanted the front page of the Daily News to read ERIC BUHARP SITS

IN SHANNON SNYDER'S GRANNY'S LIVING ROOM AND DRINKS A COKE!!!! I Thought it was news worthy, and just wait until I can tell Lynn!

Years went on and so did life. Just like all of us, I had experiences, made mistakes, and so did he. At age 19, I married and soon after divorced. Somewhere in there over the years Eric had given an engagement ring or two to a few potentially lucky girls, but none of those relationships panned out. Life is so unpredictable, but God had plans.

Chapter 3: Trip to Texas

In the Spring of 1994, after my divorce, the telephone rang in my one-bedroom apartment. The voice said "Is Shannon there?"

I replied "This is Shannon." When he responded "This is Eric," my mind raced. I knew only ONE Eric. THE ERIC, but I calmly said "Eric who?" "This is Eric Buharp" the voice answered. SWEET MOTHER OF GOD IT'S HIM!!!

He wanted to know if I could come hang out at Texas, a country western bar in Ft. Walton, with a group of them that weekend. I told him I wasn't sure. I had a boyfriend at the time, but I would see. Now, the devil himself could

not have kept me away from Texas that
weekend, so there I went. As I walked in, I
saw him in the back near the pool tables. He
had been playing pool but had taken a break.
He had his chair leaned back on two legs, his
own legs propped up and crossed on the
table in front of him, rocking himself
back and forth. Damn, why does he have to be
so good looking? The first thing he said
to me so calmly and confidently was
 "If you'll date me, I will make you the queen
of my double wide trailer."
  I will never forget those words for as long
as I live. God knows how much I wanted that
to come true one day, but staying true to my
inner 8th grader in the mirror, I said to him

"maybe one day, but for now I truly am dating someone." I stayed a while longer, but eventually goodbye. Time marched on.

Through the years Sammy Kersaw sang softly in the back of my head "so I made her the queen of my double wide trailer with the polyester curtains and the red wood deck. Sometimes she runs and I've got to trail her dagger black heart and her pretty redneck."

Chapter 4: God Has Plans

In the summer of 1994, I decided on a whim it would be a good idea to move to Alabama with the aforementioned boyfriend and have a fresh start. That didn't last long for a variety of reasons, and before I knew it, I was back in Florida. It was October, and I was more than glad to be back in the sunshine state. No offense Alabama, but I left no happy memories.

February 8, 1995, I was living in a single wide trailer on Pine Street in Seminole. One afternoon my phone rang. "Hello. Is Shannon there?" "This is Shannon." "This is Eric." Lord Jesus in heaven, maker of all things good and Holy, is this really him?

Testing God, faith, and all that is right in the
universe I say "Eric who?" He says "Eric
Buharp. I heard you are single and was
wondering if you would like to go to a
wedding with me as my date?" WELL
SWEET BABY JESUS DOES A MONKEY
LOVE BANANAS? I respond in my best
I-am- not- going- to-freak-out voice "Oh, that
sounds good. I would love to."

February 10, 1995, at 23 years old, I
have my first adult date with Eric
Buharp. He wanted us to get together before
the wedding to spend some time and get to
know each other. From February 10 on we did

not spend much time apart except for work and one trip for him hunting in Pennsylvania. I was and still am a nurse at a hospital in Niceville, Florida. He was working in the maintenance department at what was then called Okaloosa Walton College. Over the years he had moved up the ladder due to his personality and hard work ethic. Everyone loved him there and still do to this day.

That year he and his brother, Matt, bought property in a little town north of Niceville, a town with no red light called Paxton. This venture was originally called B&B Trees Farms, then later named The Paxton project.

Chapter 5: The Paxton Project

These two brothers envisioned living
outside the city limits of the ever-growing
Niceville. They wanted to live in the country
on a dirt road away from most people
and just enjoy life at a little slower pace. I will
never forget the first time we loaded
up in Eric's truck. He had somewhere he
wanted to show me. It seemed like the longest
ride of my life to nowhere. I remember
asking him once I arrived at the recently
clear-cut property for the first time "Can we
get back to Niceville from here?" There were
times I would grow to hate the isolation of

this place. In my late twenties I thought the seclusion would kill me. Little did I know that for the next 20 years I would make that drive twice a day to and from work and grow to love and be drawn to a little piece of land on Sandy Ramp Road. In my 40s, I have learned this solitude gives me peace and restores my soul. It keeps my memories alive and give my dreams space to grow, but I am getting ahead of myself.

Since February 1995, Eric and I did not spend much time apart. I stayed with him in Paxton, or he stayed with me in the little single wide trailer until, one day, he asked me to move in with him. My response "Now you don't think you are going to get me to come live up there in the middle of nowhere with you forever and never be married. I am NOT moving to Paxton unless there is a ring in my future!" My inner 13-year old would be so proud of my boldness with him! He just laughed and said of course that was in the plan. Needless to say, to be with him, I happily moved to a little place called Paxton.

Chapter 6: Magical (sort of)

In the spring of 1996 we took a trip to Disney World. Like for many others, this is my favorite place on earth. We had the time of our lives: the shows, the rides, the Dole whips, and turkey legs. On day two of the Disney trip we decided to go back to the Magic Kingdom, even though we had just been there the day before.

We had this Disney thing figured out, and I had done A LOT of studying on the subject. We approached the park clockwise, first through Adventureland, hitting the Pirates of the Caribbean, looping back around to the

Jungle Boat Cruise, the Tiki Birds, then taking a walk up the Swiss Family Tree House. We would go on to Frontier Land, Liberty Square, Fantasy Land, Mickey's Toon Town, then finally, Tomorrowland with the last ride usually being Space Mountain.

We are on PTC, one of our favorite rides, and as we are about to go down the flume hearing "Dead Men Tell No Tales" I put my hand on his leg close to his pocket. I felt something. I asked what it was. He said "Oh, it is just a couple of park maps I had folded up and stuck there" and that was that. We had a blast and closed the park down for the second day in a row.

We got back to the hotel only to have him

rush to the bathroom. We will leave it at that.
I would find out he had been nervous
all day trying to figure out how to ask me
THE QUESTION. When he came out of the
bathroom, and all I will say is there was a
paint peeling kind of smell coming from that
area. He then says "Go look in your make up
bag. What is that laying on top?" The make-
up bag is, of all places, in that bathroom. I
told him "I don't know, but I can certainly
wait for the situation in that bathroom to clear
up to find out. He pleads "No really. Go look
now." I held my breath, rushed into the
bathroom, grabbed up a little box that was
sitting on top of my make-up bag, and rushed
back out of there before I had to come up for

air. I sat back down on the bed bedside him with the box in my hand.

He takes the box, gets down on one knee, and asks me to marry him. ERIC BUHARP IS ASKING ME TO MARRYING HIM the little 7th grader inside me is yelling! I threw my arms around his neck and exclaimed "Yes, yes!" I then teased him about all the more appropriate, magical places he could have asked me to marry him on a Disney vacation like in front of Cinderella's Castle, by the teacups, or hell, even on the sidewalk near the bakery on Mainstreet U.S.A., instead of a hotel room near a bathroom that he had just recently ruined for hours. He said he had been so nervous all day and when I had asked what was in his pocket on the pirates ride he just knew he had been busted. He explained he tried all day long to ask me, but his nerves just wouldn't bring him to do it.   It didn't matter anyway. I WAS GOING TO MARRY ERIC BUHARP.

Chapter 7: Plans of a Lifetime

We planned our wedding and honeymoon while living in Paxton. I remember on one particular occasion making honeymoon plans while planting pine tree saplings from a sack draped over my shoulder as he walked ahead of me with a dibble. A dibble is a tool to make holes in the ground. He would poke holes, and I would drop the little tree in, roots down, needles up, then cover the hole back in with dirt with the help of my foot.

On this little lonely road called Sandy Ramp

we had cook outs, mud bogs, mud fights, and made memories we are still talking about over 20 years later.

"Remember the time on Leon's birthday weekend when Domnic started the procession of trucks getting stuck in the wet weather pond? He got his own truck stuck then one by one, in a true display of Busch Light and testosterone, Eric, Tim, Kenny, and Jody not only did NOT get Domnic pulled out, but got their own trucks stuck too?" Matt and Leon did not get involved initially. They sat back on a toolbox and watched the whole spectacle from afar. I few cold ones later, full of ego and optimism, they too got in their own trucks and tried to help out. They had both those trucks stuck too in less than 30 seconds, Leon in less than a half inch of mud. They would later have to put their tails between their legs and call Chris Ely to come pull everyone out of that goopy mud the next day.

So many of these crazy stories we still talk about so many years later. They never get old, and we will still be talking about them for years to come.

We planned the wedding for September 21, 1996. My dad had kindly encouraged us not to have the wedding during hunting season. For some, planning life around "doe days" or when the bucks "rut" is a big thing.

September could not get here fast enough. I would discover later there were not many

things in my life I would ever be sure.
Marrying Eric would always be on that short
list of things I was certain of in my lifetime.
We had the wedding in the backyard of my
dad and stepmom's home. My colors were
maroon and country blue. I bought my off-
white, tea-length dress off the rack at JC
Penney in the mall for $100.00. It was the
first one I tried on. I fell in love with the look
and the price. The bridesmaids' dresses ran
about $20-25 at either JC Penney or Kmart, of
all places. Now this little piece of
information about cost may seem trivial to
some, but if you know anything at all about
me, you know the cost of things is a BIG deal
to me. If you happen to compliment me on a

shirt or dress I am wearing, I am horrible about humbly and graciously accepting the compliment. I truly lack the ability to simply say "thank you" and move on. I have a compulsion to blurt out to you that I bought it just yesterday at Beall's Outlet. I will go on to tell you it was a blue dot clearance item, and I only paid $2.90 for the damn thing. I just cannot help myself. Anyway, back to the point, the wedding.

September 21, 1996 had arrived! The most awaited day of my life up to that point had come! The sky drizzled rain that morning as my granny and aunt fixed my hair in my granny's beauty shop. That hair was teased, pulled, poofed, and sprayed so much that gale force winds could not have affected that hair-do. I am honestly shocked my hair has moved to this day. We prayed the rain would stop and, just like so many blessings it did. Just about 30 minutes before our service, The clouds literally moved away, and the sun gently peaked out around them, almost giggling.

I heard the wedding procession music start to play as my dad and I linked arm in arm. We walked from his garage around the corner to their back deck where the wedding party waited. There he was. There was the boy that had worn the braces from that Ruckel dance. Oh, how I wanted to run up to him, jump up in his arms, and say "Yes, yes! Of course, I will marry you!" but, I knew we had to get through the formalities of the service first, OUR service.

Finally, the pastor said "Do you Shannon take Eric to be your lawful, wedded husband, in sickness and in health, forsaking all others for as long as you both shall live so help you God?" I trembled and answered "I do." He then announced "Eric you may kiss your bride," and the rest is history. At the reception, we danced our first dance as husband and wife to Neil McCoy's song "No Doubt About It". "Just like every lock has got to have a key. Every river flows looking for the sea, and when you plant a seed, it reaches for the sky. That's just the way it is. Nobody wonders why. Like coffee needs a cup, you know that it ain't no good without it. We were meant to be together, no doubt about it." That's right Neil. There really was no doubt about it.

   Now back to the vows for a minute. I remember vividly during his sermon, the pastor talking about how a man must leave his mother and father and cling to his wife. Leave and cleave. Ok, I get it. I can do that. In addition, he had us repeat after him saying "I, Eric, bequeath you Shannon with my trough." Now I am not really sure what that means, but what I took it to mean is "what's mine is mine and what's his is mine." I would remind him of our wedding vows many times over the next 11 years when we were having a

"discussion." I would say to him "You can't say that to me.

You bequeathed me with your trough!" He would always let me win. When he did, he would really be the one winning, as I just fell for him more and more with each passing year.

Chapter 8: Baby Makes Three

In September-October of 1997, I was kneeling over a flowerbed at our home, digging deep into the soil to plant my flowers. I developed terrible heartburn. As I could remember, I had never had heartburn before. I remember thinking to myself "Do I either have stomach cancer and by chance am dying or could I possibly be pregnant?!"

I drove up to the Piggly Wiggly in Florala, Alabama and bought a little home pregnancy test. I got back home and nervously proceeded to take the test. The results were positive! Eric wasn't home from work yet, so I had to save the test. I called and told him I had something to tell and show him when he got home. I displayed the little stick to him when he arrived, without really having to "explain" anything at all. Without a glove or anything, he grabbed that thing up and took off running! I yelled "Wait! Where are you going with that? You do know I peed on that, right?" With a beaming smile he replied "I'm putting it in my truck to take it to work tomorrow to show everyone!" "Um. Ok. Let me at least put that in a baggie for you so no one else accidently touches it."

On May 4, 1998, Jessie Hunter Buharp, the most amazing little human I had ever laid my eyes on was born. Weighing 8 pounds even, he looked like a tiny cherub. As they took our

son to get his first bath, I made Eric follow
the nurse holding him and instructed him to
keep his eyes on that baby, if no more than
through the nursery window. I didn't want my
little one switched accidentally with anyone
else's and sending his daddy to guard him
assured me that didn't happen. I wanted that
tiny baby boy with me every second that they
didn't absolutely need him in the nursery.
When they picked the baby up each time to
take him to see the doctor, I wanted to know
"How long will you have him? When will you
be bringing him back?" I would later come to
the solid realization that this attachment only
grows and intensifies over the years, even
when that 8-pound baby is 20 years old, is

6'1", and weighs 210 pounds.

Chapter 9: The Circle is Complete

We always knew we wanted two children. That was a given. The planner that I was, I even knew how old I wanted Hunter to be when he got a brother or sister. I knew I wanted him to be able to walk, talk, feed himself, and be potty-trained before we started all over again with all that a baby entails. I also knew the time of year I wanted to be my biggest pregnant self. I did not want to be as big as a whale in August. In June-July 2001, we got the news we were expecting again. Excited was an understatement. I initially envisioned a girl and fell head over hills for the song "My

Maria" by Brooks and Dunn. That would be "her" name, Maria Christine. "My Maria, don't you know I've come a long, long way. I've been longing to see her. When she's around she takes my blue away."

The ultrasound to determine the sex of the baby confirmed this would not be Maria. We saw a "turtle" on the ultrasound indicating a boy, rather than a "hamburger", which would have meant a girl. I have to say I was a little bit sad I would not have a Maria, but truly relieved because I knew how to be the mom of a boy.

This birth would make Eric a father again, the dad of TWO boys. He was so very nervous. Before wheeling me into the O.R. for the C-section, the nurse had to help him get dressed in scrubs over his clothes. He fumbled as he couldn't get dressed quickly or well. His shoelaces had become untied, and she even had to help re-tie them for him. Seemed he even lacked the coordination in his fingers to do this menial task.

Wyatt Cade Buharp arrived on the scene March 8, 2002. He was the tiniest little baby a had ever been up close to. He weighed 6 pounds, 3 ounces and, compared to the images of baby Hunter in my mind, he seemed so very small. I had honestly worried during pregnancy if I could possibly love this baby as much as the first one. The first time I held that precious boy in my arms

I had a new appreciation for the capacity of a heart to love. My heart swelled and literally divided completely in two. I now think I get the concept of how atoms split. My family was now complete. I had my Eric and my two precious boys. Cade somehow managed to grab both the loose ends of my circle of love, tie them together, and make the circle complete.

Chapter 10: Life, Adventures, and Memories

I have to say we were a happy family, and the center of that family was the two of us. We were a true team. I always told Eric if something happened to me he could pick up the pieces without missing a beat, even when the boys were babies. Really, he could do most things better than I could. We even use to argue in the middle of the night about who would get up with the crying baby, bantering back and forth while rising up out of bed to a sitting position. "No, I will get up and get him this time." "No, you lay here and rest, I will get him this time." Most times we would get up together and sleepily walk to the crib of one of our little wailing sons. Actually, we sometimes had little slapping matches with each other on who would lean down and pick up the baby. The only thing that comes to mind is an episode of the Three Stooges.

Even when our boys were babies and toddlers, we camped many places. We pulled Radio Flyer wagons around campgrounds with babies propped up on pillows and stuffed animals. We changed diapers on towels laid down on trails. We held diaper bags, sippy cups, and pushed strollers throughout Disney World, Gatlinburg, Chattanooga, and St. Augustine.

We packed so much happiness, joy, love, and memories in to what we didn't know would be the little time we had.

I never understood the thinking behind people who won't travel or vacation while they have babies and toddlers. Clearly you have never seen the expression on a 1-year old's face when he is sitting in your lap on a ferry boat through It's a Small World with all the lights and dolls with flashy, sequined outfits. The dolls dance in circles and happy animals pop up and down from all around. Many peoples don't know that, in many ways, you have the advantage while pushing a stroller through the Magic Kingdom. Insider tip: a Disney rental stroller, especially a double one, sounds like a herd of buffalo coming across the bridge from Main Street U.S.A. over into Adventureland and people WILL move.

I remember once at Disney's Animal Kingdom Cade was approximately 10-months old. He was still drinking from a bottle. I know that. We had just taken the train from Harambe, Africa over to Rafiki's Planet Watch. Cade had just finished a bottle of formula. He then was placed over Eric's shoulders when we got off the train, so he could be up high and see all the animals in the petting zoo. It was a hot summer day. This heat was mixed with a baby whose belly was full, jostling up and down on his daddy's shoulders. We were standing near the Affection Section, which is the petting zoo. We were right by the goats when little Cade's stomach could take no more. He puked right on top of Eric's head, chunks of clabbered milk dripping down his head, eyes, and cheeks. These drops of goop seemed to be racing down his face to drip to the pavement. First there was shock by both of us, then a little laughter. I gave baby Cade to grandma and rushed Eric into the empty women's rest room where we attempted to wash his hair at the sink. These memories still make me smile, snicker and warm my heart.

Chapter 11: God Bless Daddy's Tallywacker

Eric had a vasectomy when Cade was still a toddler. We had already decided two children was what we wanted, as well as what we could afford. We decided he would get a vasectomy, as I had already been under the knife twice for C-sections. I explained to him it was basically his "turn".

We arrived at the physician's office for the procedure. Eric got up on the table, draped and prepped when the doctor recognized me from the hospital. He numbed Eric's "area of interest" while talking to me about things going on at the hospital like who still worked there, who had left, and any other gossip we could think of.

Meanwhile, he has Eric's procedural area in his hands and starts snipping, clipping, and clamping. Eric got tired of this conversation that he is not a part of after a while, and reminded me and the good doctor where the focus should be, precisely between his legs. The rest of the procedure was completed quietly.

I got his pain medication filled and gave him a dose. By the time we were in Mossy Head life was good for Eric. Everything was funny. This comedy of damn near everything was short lived as by the next morning his "scrotal area" was almost the size of a number

4 soccer ball.

Cade was too little to understand, but Hunter could see there was something wrong in daddy's "tallywacker" area just by the way daddy walked.

A few days later was Thanksgiving. Eric Was still moving slowly and carefully. There we all are in my granny's dining room, surrounded by the wonderful aromas of the delicious food, as well as the nicely decorated table with tablecloth in place. Hunter was encouraged to say grace and bless the meal before we started eating. He was 5 years old. He gave thanks for the turkey, mashed potatoes, and macaroni and cheese, then wrapped it up with asking God to bless and help his daddy's tallywacker get better very soon. It was a very nice prayer.

Chapter 12: NOT Miss Fix-It

Looking back, I wish I had learned how to do so much more such as fixing things, using a saw, repairing a toilet, sink, or hanging a ceiling fan. He never would even let me repaint a room. He would set a chair out for me to sit in, then he would get to painting. My painting is horrible now. I get paint on the ceiling, carpet, and especially on my clothes, hair, and face. I just never had to learn.

Anytime I would offer to help with manual labor, Eric would say "you just sit there and be beautiful and I will do it."

These days I have to be humble and ask for help for things I don't know how to fix: plumbing problems, septic tank issues, washer or dryer won't work, or when we have no water in the house. I HATE, absolutely loathe, having to ask for help. Eric never taught me how to work on the vehicles, use a skill saw to repair the porches, or fix that damn lawnmower. He always assumed he would be here to do all those tasks. I hate that damn lawnmower.

Chapter 13: Writing Our Story

We talked by phone each day on the way home from work, catching up on the day's activities. We actually had conversations and heard each other's voices. We didn't text back then. When we would talk by phone, sometimes I would start off with "What's going on?" He would usually come back with "Nothing but you baby."

Over the years, we would see so many relationships try and fail. Ours came so easily that it was hard to understand the problems. We would even sit and talk on the porch sometimes about the issues others were facing, shake our heads in sadness and talk about a book we were going to write together one day about marriage and staying together. He would say "I just don't know what is going on with them Babygirl." We were truly blessed or had somehow gotten lucky and figured out a formula for success in life and love. By this point, I truly could not imagine my life without him in it.

Since Eric has moved to heaven I still remember the conversations about our book. Don't worry Eric. I am going to write our story one day, I promise.

Chapter 14: Forever Home on Earth

In 2000, we sold our mobile home in Paxton and had it moved off our property, but we still had the land. We had a home built in Mossy Head, a little township closer to each of our jobs. I thought I had to get closer to Niceville and people. It was a beautiful house, those memories I cherish.

I am not ashamed to say, most anything I wanted I got. We had been talking about my having the opportunity to be a stay-at-home mom for a while with Cade, as I had not been able to with Hunter. Again, Eric just said whatever I wanted, he would figure it out.

Finally, in 2005 the housing market boomed. We never were wealthy people. We were definitely blue collar, but we got by comfortably. We even had plans, some that Eric would write down in algorithm format (because he knew I liked that), so we could see those goals in black and white. We wanted to be debt-free: no house payments, no vehicle payments, and we also had planned to have our funerals paid off before we were 40 years old. We did all that, even paying for the funerals. His by immediate need. I would go within a few months after he went to heaven back to the very same funeral home and pay for mine.

I was 36 years old and had already planned my funeral. Some may find it morbid. I call it proper planning and being organized. Ultimately, it gave me peace. I am a control freak, and I want to tell you what songs to play, in what order, the format of the service, and there will probably even be instructions on what to eat afterward for the social, or where I would like for you to go out to eat, but I don't want to spoil all the fun or mystery. If you are dying to know, there is a folder in the top of my file cabinet labeled "My Funeral". Make sure you follow my instructions when the time comes, or I won't be happy.

We were able to sell our home for double

what we paid for it. After we paid off the existing house, and it was all said and done, we had $50,000.00 to build our house back in Paxton on the land where the double wide trailer used to sit. Seems we were right back to square one. The little front yard patiently waited all those years for our return.

We lived in Eric's parents' camper while he, along with family and friends, helped build our home. Eric would work all day at the college in Niceville, then come home every evening and work on the house until 9 or 10 pm, go to bed, then get up and do it all again the next day. He worked endlessly.

Now mind you, I was not working now. I

was a stay-at-home mom alone with a 3-year old in a camper. There were days he would come in from work, grab a bite to eat, and I would put my head down on the table in the camper and cry saying "I don't know how much more of this I can take. This small space is killing me! I am going to go crazy in this camper!"

I can see his dilemma. He had a house to work on and a wife losing her mind. He would tell me "I don't know whether to stay in here, console you and calm you down, or get on out there to the house and hammer a few nails so we can get that house finished." I would wipe tears, slobber, snot, and assure him I would be okay, and out the camper door he would go over to our future home and get to work. I believe the footer was dug for the little house in October of 2005 and by March of 2006 we were moving in. Pretty good for a man with no contractor, a full- time job, building it himself with the help of family and friends at night and on weekends.

Now I cannot see ever leaving this little house. It is small, modest, humble, and not flashy at all. It is basic and without any bells or whistles, but I know every crack in the tile, chip in the paint, and root in the yard. This little home has a pulse that beats rhythmically with my very own heartbeat.

Chapter 15: April 2007

One afternoon in April 2007, I had just gotten Hunter home from school. Eric should have been arriving home soon with Cade, who now attended VPK a few days a week in Niceville just for socialization. My house phone rang. It was a dispatcher with, I believe, either the sheriff's department or highway patrol. This woman informed me that my husband and preschooler had been involved in a vehicle accident in New Harmony. I asked her what the location was. She gave it to me. I told her "I am going to give you my cell phone number now and hang up. I am going to my husband and my baby."

She encouraged me not to do so, but I didn't hear the rest. I had already hung up the phone and was out the door with Hunter by the hand.

As we came up on the scene, I saw Eric standing outside the car that was smashed on one side. I heard my baby screaming loudly and then there was silence. I let Hunter stand with a trusted young lady nearby and ran to my littler son. Eric was so shaken, but I couldn't focus on him now. Our little one needed me. The screams alternating with silence continue. They got Cade in the ambulance. I got in right with him.

A Ford F-350 had run a stop sign and plowed right into my family's car. Cade was in the back seat in his car seat. On impact his little face hit hard against the hard, plastic part of the door underneath the window. This fractured the bone around his left eye and caused an open wound on his left cheek that would require surgery.

In the ambulance, his heart rate would be elevated when he was screaming. I know he was screaming out of pain and fear. He would then become silent, and his heart rate would drop very low. He was trying to pass out from the trauma and pain of it all. He was 4 years old. It killed me as I watched him and his heart rate intently and continuously. I would rub his sternum to get him to wake back up.

Then the screams would come again.

The EMT in the ambulance assured me I was doing the right thing. I am a mommy right now, not a nurse. I need all the help I can get. I can't think very well.

We made it to the hospital in Crestview, where we were quickly Life-flighted to Sacred Heart in Pensacola. Not long after we arrived, Cade was in surgery to repair the wound to his face and evaluate his left eye. This tough little boy made it out of surgery just fine. Eric had no injuries except a very sore arm from the air bag deployment. God is so good ALL THE TIME. My little family was still intact. To this day, Cade has a scar to his left cheek that looks like a backward "C". We have always told him it is a "C" for Cade, just like "Z" for Zorro.

Chapter 16: The Day that Changed Absolutely Everything

Friday July 11, 2008 was a day full of excitement and anticipation. We had a day full of fun planned. I had a unit meeting at work at 07:30. Eric went on in to his job to do some paperwork too, taking the two boys with him. He had just received another job promotion. I cannot remember the exact title, but I believe it was assistant director of the physical plant at what was then called Okaloosa Walton College.

Our boys were 6 and 10 years old at the time. They were so excited about the pirate cruise we would be going on in Panama City later in the day. Eric dropped me off at work then went on to his. I am not sure to this day how much paperwork he got done with the boys there, but I know he didn't mind.

He picked me back up at 08:30, and we headed for Panama City. We stopped at McDonald's in Niceville on the way out of town. Can you believe I remember what he had to eat: two breakfast burritos with mild sauce, a hash brown, and a Coke. Funny what you remember.

We boarded the Sea Dragon Pirate Cruise at the appointed time. Along with other kids, the boys swabbed the deck, heard pirate tales, got mustaches painted on them, wore bandanas and beads, and we all got to sightsee around

St. Andrews Bay. I took a picture of Eric and the boys as the ship was sailing out. I would never dream in a thousand years this would be the last picture I would ever take of my amazing husband together with our two precious boys. I would days later look back at the camera and see that he had taken several pictures of me. I had had no idea. I cannot express how looking at those pictures of me through his eyes makes me feel loved.

After the cruise, we were hungry and ate at a little restaurant near the ship. I think it had an appropriate nautical theme. I remember sitting there looking at my little family, Eric smiling and helping the boys with their food, the boys chattering and being busy as little boys do at the table. In that moment I asked them "Do you have any idea how lucky we all are? I have a husband who loves me and I love more than anything. Boys, you have parents that love you beyond measure, and a mommy and daddy who love each other just as much. We are so very blessed." I don't know why I was compelled to say that, but I meant every single word and still do. Honestly, the word blessed was an understatement.

Traveling back home that afternoon, I recall a song that came on the radio. It was Jack Johnson singing "Upside Down", a song from the movie *Curious George*.

I had always said this was our little family's

song and announced that once again as the song played. I sang along with Jack "Upside down, I'll find the things they say just can't be found. I'll share this love I have with everyone. I'll sing and dance to mother nature's songs. I don't want this feeling to go away."

Traveling back home from Panama City to Paxton, we stopped in the parking lot of the Defuniak Walmart where we picked up Lynn's daughter, Katie. Yes, the same Lynn from Jr. High School. Yes, we are still friends. She somehow forgave me for gabbing about Eric so much back then. Katie was 10 years old, the same age as Hunter. She was spending the weekend with us, as Lynn was a nurse too and had to work 12-hour shifts at the hospital that weekend. We got Katie in the car. Cade was sitting behind Eric, Katie in the middle, and Hunter behind me. Of course, I was in the passenger's seat.

I have always wondered how things might have been different if we had just stayed 5 minutes longer talking to Lynn and exchanging Katie and her weekend belongings from one vehicle to the other. Maybe we would have never even been near the scene of the wreck.

We are traveling on a county road headed toward home. The kids were talking amongst themselves in the backseat, and I was talking to Eric about what we were going to do for supper, maybe hamburgers, except I didn't have any hamburger meat laid out to thaw.

We see a semi-truck rounding a corner and losing control. It started tipping on its side and sliding toward us. The scene in my mind is still like something from an action movie.

Disbelief is the only word that comes to mind. I hear Eric say "Oh, my God. Oh, my God" as he tries to move off the road into the ditch to our right. The last thing I remember thinking is "we are going to die." This thought was not filled with panic or anxiety. There was no time for that. Just the simple realization that we were going to die and that was that. Then IMPACT.

Then there was silence. When I opened my eyes I truly thought I might have died and was now in the hereafter. When I realized I was still alive, I couldn't look immediately to my left at Eric. I was afraid of what I might find. I looked directly in the back to the kids. They all are alive. I got out and open Hunter's door.

I try to be calm with them while unbuckling each seat belt but am telling them "get out" "get out". I was afraid the car might catch on fire. I had to get them to safety. I wasn't thinking about possible injuries at this time. There was one objective. Get the kids out of the car. I would later be told that Katie heard Hunter tell Cade "Cade, I don't think daddy is going to make it" while they were still in the car. I helped each one out and moved them as far away from the vehicle as I can. I didn't know I sat them in an ant bed. Praise God they were alive and safe though. I now can get back to Eric.

As I came back to the scene, I could see he was able to move the vehicle off the road into a ditch so much so that his driver side front of the car took most of the hit. He had literally maneuvered the car so that he took all the force. This is just like him, always sacrificing himself where we are concerned. I slid back into the passenger seat to see him. His sweet head was slumped over, eyes closed, and he was breathing deep with an irregular pattern.

I knew we may be dealing with some brain trauma. I put my hands to his face and tried to hold his head up straighter, hoping he could breathe a little easier. I kept telling him again over and over "Eric I love you so much. Please don't leave me. I love you. I need you, please don't leave me!" I only wanted him to hear two things: How much I love him and begging him not leave me, hoping somewhere in the back of his consciousness he could hear me. I know if there was any way he could speak to me he would tell me he loves me too, and he is trying very hard to stay.

Several people stuck their face in Eric's window, talking to me to encourage me to get out of the car. I AM NOT LEAVING

MY ERIC I Scream in my head. HE IS MINE. Finally, a familiar face peeps in his window. It was my friend Melanie Howard. She is a paramedic, and I had known her from the hospital. I felt a slight sense of relief. I felt comfortable with her helping Eric. She put her own hands on his head to help support him then looked at me and told me kindly, gently that I need to get out of the car now so she can better help him. I look in her eyes, and I know she KNOWS how much he means to me. I know she will do absolutely all she can to help Eric.

Some friends, Justin and Amy Davis, happened upon the scene. They had taken Hunter, Cade, and Katie to their van to keep them safe. Coincidentally, I would learn later that Amy shares the same birthday as Eric. Justin's birthday is the day Eric entered heaven. They would also come to the hospital that the boys and I were at and stay until late into the night.

Finally, the MAST helicopter arrives. They had removed Eric from the car with the jaws of life. Up the helicopter went with Eric, Katie, my heart, hopes, and future with it.

The boys and I were then taken by ambulance to a nearby hospital, where we were evaluated overnight for any hidden injuries. Hunter had a broken foot, and each of the boys had seat beat abrasions across their abdomens, which they wanted to watch for possible injuries. Eric and Katie were taken to South East Alabama Medical Center in Dothan. Lynn was with them. I would find out Katie was then transferred to UAB Children's Hospital as she required surgery on her back and abdomen from injuries she sustained. Lynn later told me she had to take off the headset they had given her in the MAST helicopter. She just couldn't take any longer hearing the medical team as they talked back and forth about Eric's injuries and probable outcome.

The boys and I were evaluated in the ER at the local hospital. We were laid on stretchers next to each other. I could keep my eyes on them and knew they were okay. My family was there in the ER with me, like a tribe. Everyone needs a tribe. Eric's parents and brother Matt traveled to Dothan to be with Eric. I cannot imagine the pain they went through. I should have been there with him too, but Eric and I always divided and conquered when it concerned the boys. He couldn't be there, so I had to follow our sons. They were shocked and scared by this horrible event and trying to process the images in their little minds.

Waiting in that ER seemed like forever, and I begged often for someone to give me an update on Eric. I felt like there was a conspiracy to keep information from me. I knew his injuries were bad. I rejected the idea that he would not make it. In my mind I calmed myself by thinking thoughts like "It will be ok. Even if he is paralyzed, you can take care of him at home. Even if he has some brain damage, you will still have your Eric and can hold his hand and talk to him. As long as he lives, you can handle anything. As long as I have my Eric back, it will be okay, and I will take him back in any form that God will give him back to me in."

The accident was around 6 pm. At around 10 pm, they wheeled me by wheelchair into a "quiet room" off the ER where my family sat. I did not have any injuries except a broken toe. There really was no need for the wheelchair. My dad had been waiting for one of the pastors of his church to deliver the news to me. With tears in his eyes and voice choked up, my dad told me Eric had not made it. Everything was in slow motion. My world stopped. I heard what he said, but my brain would not process it.

Eric's mom and dad arrived at the hospital. They had just lost their son, but they came to check on the boys and me. I remember walking up to Mrs. B and just hugging her so tight, trying to find some comfort from my husband's mother. She had just lost her son, but I needed to hold her and feel her holding me because she had given my husband life. She is truly the strongest woman I know and through her shock and grief, she comforted me. The staff took the boys and I into a room all together on the pediatric ward. Our little boys laid together on one small bed. I sat at the foot of their bed, held them, and sometimes just watched them. I was already wondering what Eric was doing at that moment and not wanting to think about being a single parent yet. My dad stayed with me that night. He sat up in a chair bedside the bed all night. My world had officially changed. My life as I knew it was now over. I would go into self-preservation mode. The new life I would be entering would be a world without color.

Chapter 17: A World without Color

Much of the days and months to come are a blur. I remember some things, others I don't. The boys and I stayed at Eric's parents' house for a while after the accident. I didn't have the heart or strength yet to go home without him. I later even went as far as renting a little house in Niceville for a few months and even enrolled the boys in school in Niceville. As of July 12, 2008, I had become an instant single parent.

With the help of Mr. and Mrs. B, we planned Eric's service. I sat up one night all night writing his obituary. I spoke at his service. I had to. Again, this is MY Eric.

There is still so much I wanted to talk to everyone about when it concerns him.

They say the line was out the door of the funeral home for the viewing and the next day for the service. I wouldn't know. I didn't leave his side much. I had to be close to him. He was lying in a casket, still, quiet, but he is still my Eric. I knew after the service I didn't have much more time to touch him, feel his skin, his hair, or touch his face. I knew when they closed that casket I would not see his beautiful face again until I was done here on this earth. That might be a while. I used my time wisely.

Hunter was in boy scouts at the time. His boy scout troop came in full uniform. The

Walton Guard did as well. This is a civil war re-enactment group that Eric was involved in. They presented a flag to Mr. B, marched in formation, presented arms, and played Taps by trumpet. Eric, I am sure, was happy and very appreciative everyone came. I can't help but feel he may have been still a little dazed by all of the events of the last week as well.

Cade would start first grade and Hunter fifth grade a month after. Nothing was the same. The sky wasn't the same color. Food didn't taste the same. Nothing was right in the world. I was scared to death but couldn't show it. Our little boys' world had just changed too. I had to show a strong back bone, at least to them. A few nights after the accident I was missing him so very much I ached to talk with him. I fell asleep dreaming he was kissing me. I remember little Cade walking up to the bedside where I was sleeping. He said "Mommy, are you kissing daddy?" I woke myself up making puckering gestures with my lips. "Yes, baby. I guess mommy was." Now I missed him more than ever. I had to talk to him SOON. Everything remained so colorless.

Chapter 18: Making Contact

First Contact 7/21/08: I got the name of a highly recommended medium and called her the next day. I set up a time to have a phone consultation with her. She was in another state. The next night at the assigned time, I called her. The following is an excerpt from that conversation. First, she told me do not give her information. She would talk to me. She did not want me feeding her any information.

She tells me I am surrounded by a lot of trauma, I am holding it in, but I want to explode. She says there is a lot of love coming to me from all directions: from the physical and the spiritual world. She describes

me as an active, very busy woman. I have to

be constantly involved in something and that

there is caretaking in my path. Then she says

"You are a nurse. I see a white uniform. You

care for children. You are in a male

dominated household. You are facing the

end of a cliff. You are looking down saying

'How am I going to get across? How

am I going to go on?' You have pathways that

have been broken."

She then says "There is a gentleman

reaching out from the spirit world. He has

recently crossed. He is strong, nice looking,

brown hair, nice features, fantastic

personality, and he is already trying to joke

with you. He is wanting you to cheer up. There is love just pouring out from him. His first question is 'How are the boys?'" She says "You and he have two boys together. This is your husband." He is telling her to tell me "Everything is fine. We went through it together. WE ARE STILL GOING THROUGH IT TOGETHER. AND YOU ARE NOT ALONE." She tells me "He is adamant that he did not leave you and he wants me to tell you 'We are not apart.' He is telling me to tell you 'This is a promise. I have never broken a promise.'" She then explains "He will be permitted to be with you throughout your life and the raising of the boys. He says 'I will be there with you and you are still the love of my life. There is just a fine line between us now. Don't give up on life.'" She blurts out at this point "He is now telling me his name is Eric."

Oh, my Jesus in the heavens. He came through. It is really him. Now, I have some questions. I asked her to ask him "Did you have a lot of pain?" He replied "I left my body immediately on impact. I was not in it. I shot right out. All of the sudden I was looking down." He says the scene was a mess. He could see that. He was watching over. He recognizes there is a purpose for everything though we might not understand. He had guiding forces. They greeted him and helped him. He looked down on the whole accident. He said it was a surreal type of thing that he was not a part of. He described it "like looking at a video."

My next question was "Do you remember our day, our last Friday together?" He said he remembers emotions, the love, the sharing. He explained all the details are stored away, but the love is always there. He says his whole being is linked with mine. He says it is hard for him to put into human words, but the main thing to understand is the connection forever, for us and for the boys.

He revealed he would be seeing things on a daily basis but through different eyes. There are no distractions where he is. He said he knows I love him and "We are one. How can there be anything that can keep us apart?" He then tries to be funny "As my heart used to beat, (she says he is laughing), and as your heart is beating now, we are soul together. You know I am not articulate with words, but our souls are entwined." He says that he is still himself and then reveals he gave me a kiss goodnight last night. Cade DID see mommy kissing daddy.

I asked him "What am I supposed to do without you?" His response "We are still together, though I am here and you are there. Until the day I yank you up to me, hug you, and then will never let you go again. We will cross over together then."

He once again is adamant that we have not parted. "In some ways, we are closer because I don't have to go to work." She says he starts laughing again! This is not funny to me Eric, tears flowing down my face over a little smile. He then said I won't be able to discuss this sort of communication with everyone, but certain ones, he will come to.

Second contact 9/23/08: I called her again from a different location and a different phone number. Again, she instructs me to say nothing and to let her see who comes through. She says "There are two gentlemen here for you in spirit. Both are giving you comfort. They both are with you and are your guardians. One is your husband, and he is shedding tears for you. He says "I just want to see you smile again. Life has not ended. I am with you. Time has no bearing. It is only time. LIFE is where I am at." He tells her I have to recognize I have work still to do down here. He keeps saying I have to take care of the boys. He says "I don't want them to see a grieving mother. I want them to see their wonderful father through YOU. I am with you every day and night."

She will then tell me the second male is my paternal grandfather, my pawpaw. He is standing beside Eric, happy, and smiling telling Eric "That's our girl." My Paw Paw went to heaven in 1993. He had multiple myeloma, bone cancer.

Now, this second contact was in the evening by telephone. This is what happened that morning, then we will get back to the medium.

The boys and I were in the rental house. I really hated it and missed my home but was still gaining the strength to return to it. I was getting the boys up for school that morning. I woke 5th grade Hunter up. He got quietly up and got ready for school as I had asked him. I woke up little 1st grade Cade. When I woke him up he said "Where is my daddy?" and was looking all around the room. I told him quietly daddy had to go to heaven but is watching and taking care of us from there. He then almost yelled defiantly "I just saw my daddy. Now where is my daddy?" He knew who he saw. I tried to calm him while wiping away tears, managed to get him settled enough to go to school, with us all being rattled over this the rest of the day.

That night the medium then goes on to explain Eric a little further. She says your husband was fully aware immediately when he crossed over. He has so much knowledge about life on both sides. She then tells me "PUT ASIDE THE THOUGHT THAT HE IS GONE." He is still with me. She says he is telling her he comes to me in dreams, holds my hand. He sometimes takes both my hands in his.

She tells me "In life and death his love is so beautiful." Then she says it. "He has also appeared before your boys. The youngest just saw him with his physical eyes." She says it takes a lot of energy for those in the spirit world to materialize to the physical eye so that they can be seen. She assured me the little one had indeed seen his daddy, just like he had said.

Third contact 4/20/09: This time Eric has several key points he wants to get across. He wants the boys to know and understand that life does not end with the ending of the physical body. If they understand this early on, it will be a lot easier for them to accept and be ready for.

Now my questions again. I asked why he had to go, and I couldn't. We were supposed to grow old together, and I don't think I can live until I am old without him. He says I still have many things to do, mainly raising our boys. I asked will he really be there when my time on earth is over. He said his hand will be the first thing mine touches when I leave the body. He reminds me again he has never broken a promise.

Ch 19: Where Do We Go from Here?

This is not a self-help book. This is mine and my family's journey through what I would not wish on anyone. There are days that I am happy and find things to be joyous about. There are days I am home alone or in the car, crying my eyes out and having screaming tantrums almost 10 years later because God did not let me keep him. I am certain I will still be crying in 50 years. The passing time does not matter. He was and always will be an integral part of my life. I will grieve forever. Everyone that knew him will.

The physical plant at the college where he worked has a breakroom where they have lunch. Above the door is a plaque that announces it is the **Buharp Lounge**. There are many pictures of him on the wall. They even keep it updated from time to time with pictures of the boys.

I still think the world lacks the color it had when he was here. The sky is a little duller and the grass not quite as green, but I try to deliberately, intentionally smile more. Sometimes it is the theory of "fake it 'til you make it." I do find I like to make people laugh these days. Sometimes it is to bless someone else, sometimes it is to help me smile. I am trying. I really am.

I still dream of Eric. During the project of
writing this book, he visited me. I was
out at the mailbox at our home. He was
working out there. I walked up to him. I
somehow knew I had not seen him in a very
long time. I put my arms around him.
I "felt" him in my hands. I had to get on my
tip toes to look right in his face. I am 5'4". He
is 6'2". I SAW him, just like Cade all those
years before. I KNOW I saw him. I said "I
really, really, really love you so much." He
just smiled and said "I really, really, really
love you too." My alarm clock woke me up. I
was almost confused that I couldn't find him.
I was so disappointed that he wasn't there, but
I KNOW he had been.

As far as my boys go, over the years I have stressed about so many "boy things" I don't know how to teach them about: changing their oil, backing up to and pulling a trailer or working on their vehicle or ATV.

Nonetheless, Hunter is now 19 years old and a pre-apprentice lineman. He is so much like his daddy in temperament and features. He has a tender heart and forgives easily. He is tall, strong, handsome, and patient. He works hard and always sees his goals ahead.

Cade is 16 years old, just started driving and in the 10th grade. He is a good looking, confident young man. He is definitely not a follower. I see so much of his daddy in him. He has leadership qualities and is strong-willed. He mentions going to lineman school when he graduates too. They both work on four wheelers, trucks, and pull trailers easily, all without my help. I could not be prouder of our two boys. They are the reason my heart still beats.

I can't help but wonder how things might have been better for them if Eric and I had traded places. I love my boys beyond words but sometimes feel they would have better been served as a role model and teacher by their daddy who knew "all things boy". I still daydream about how our lives would have been so much different today if Eric had been able to stay with us. I will miss him for eternity and am grateful for every single second with him since my 7th grade year.

Katie had to have back and abdominal surgery back then. She has since had many more abdominal surgeries. She is a courageous young woman full of self-confidence and determination. She is a college student at the University of Alabama and doing very well. She knows I think she is spectacular and holds a special place in my heart.

As for myself and Lynn, we are still the best of friends. We talk about the past, present, future, and truly keep each other grounded.

Somehow, we all have managed to make it at the end of each day, though I am crying even while writing this.

Much of this story I have written from my front porch rocking chair, the very same rocking chairs where he and I used to sit and solve all life's problems, the same place we would talk about writing our book one day.

I will miss Eric all the days of my life, but me and his boys, we are going to make it. I will see to that just as he expects me to.

My life may be completely different now, nothing like I had envisioned. I am heartbroken those plans did not last as long as I had wanted, but oh, the things I got to do and be while they did.

Ch 20: What I Have Gotten to Be

Grief is a funny, steadfast entity. It can be stubborn and determined. July 11, 2018 will be 10 years that Eric has lived in heaven. I can't help but think about all that has not been able to be since his permanent address is in eternity.

I get angry, bitter, and feel selfish. I wrestle with granting forgiveness that has never even been asked for. I honestly am not there yet. I don't know that I will ever be, but that is between myself and God. I think that life can be so unfair. Sometimes you just have to allow grief the space it pleads for.

Other times I can muster up the mindset to

counterbalance it with gratefulness.

YES! I WANTED to be married for 60 + years. I wanted Eric to see his boys learn to drive, graduate high school, grow into fine young men, one day see his boys get married, hold his grandchildren, and, when I am a very old woman, with unapologetic selfishness wanted him to hold MY hand while I crossover. No one gets everything they want, so instead I compiled a list of all the things I did get just because a 9th boy with braces at a Ruckel Jr. High School dance asked ME to dance.

1. I got to be a 7th grade girl who had a crush on a 9th grade boy, leading to her first kiss.

2. When I was 23 years old, I got to be his date to a wedding.

3. I got to be queen of a double wide trailer when I was 24 years old.

4. I got to be in our own wedding later that year, getting to become a wife.

5. When I was 26 and again at age 30, I got to become a mother.

6. In 2005-2006 I got to be a construction supervisor on building a home from the ground up.

7. I got to always be right!

8. I got to be shown and told I was
   the most important person
   and loved more than anything
   in this world by one person on
   earth.
9. When I was 36 years old, I had to
   say goodbye (for just a little
   while) to the physical person I
   have adored since I was 13 years
   old.
10. Through that boy with braces, I
    have never been more certain
    that heaven exists and is more
    real than anything on this earth.

11. As I am 46 years old, I have to
    remind myself that I got to be a
    part of something some people
    never will. They can't even
    comprehend what I am talking
    about.

12. Every day I get to see Eric's
     boys grow into men with
     characteristics much like his.

13. I get to anticipate the day my
     boys will meet "the one" (when
     they are 30), and I get to see one
     very lucky girl get to make a
     mental list of all the things she
     has gotten to be because of one
     of my boys.

This life is hard, sad, difficult, and unfair. It
is also magical, beautiful, and full of so many
precious, precious gifts. Remember them.
Recognize them. SEE them.

Chapter 21: And the Dance Continues

Some never get to experience a fairytale, but I DID. It really happened to me. My school girl fantasies and young woman dreams came true! I got to LIVE that dream. I got to love and be loved like God intended-an agape, whole, heart squeezing, "so painful I can't breathe the same once it is gone" kind of love. The kind of love where I feel lost, like a part of my body is missing, and "I am not sure how to live with a gaping hole inside of me" kind of love.

My prayer is that someday each and every one of you gets to experience this kind of love in your lifetime too.

My hope is that I live to be a very old woman, at least 102, and that I am blessed with the privilege of seeing my two sons grow into GOOD men, husbands, and fathers.

It is my ambition to be a part of my grandchildren and great grandchildren's lives and be a strong influence in those little lives long after I have moved on to heaven.

It is my wish, when my time on this earth is over, that I lay down in my own bed, close my eyes and then peacefully make the cross over from this life into eternity with my circle of love surrounding me.

It is my highest aspiration during this transition to see a hand reaching out to me-that very familiar face with the hazel, twinkling eyes and beaming smile and as he holds out his hand to me, asks me to dance.......

Disney World 2004

Christmas 2002

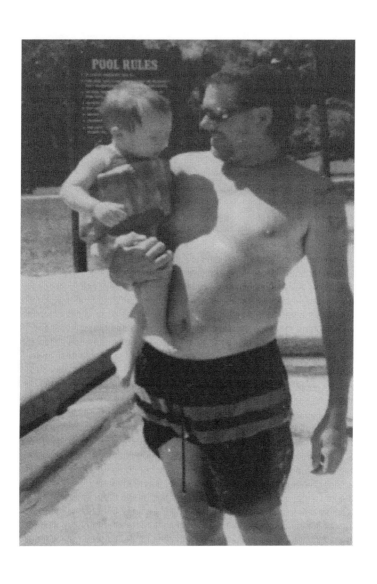

Eric & Cade at pool at Disney's Ft.
Wilderness 2003

Eric & Hunter @ Disney Buzz Lightyear
Space Ranger Spin 2003

Eric hunting in Pennsylvania winter 2005

Eric & Hunter Gatlinburg Fall 2002

Eric & Cade hunting winter 2005

Eric the starfish 2005

Our wedding September 21, 1996

Our family Christmas photo December 2006

July 11, 2008

"Love travels the miles upon the wings of angels.

Love finds you. I swear it's true.
I can love you from here.

On moonbeams, on heartstrings, love makes its way through everything.

Love finds you. I swear it's true.

I will always be near, and I'll love you from here."

Lyrics from Kathy Mattea song *Love Travels*

58831626R00081

Made in the USA
Columbia, SC
25 May 2019